"Artificial intelligence is not a threat to human creativity; it is its extension. Technology frees us from mechanical work, creating space for imagination to flourish." — Steve Jobs

2024 Copy Right: Illution Production Ida

Translation by ChatGPT 4o

illution.biz

The Talented Mr. AI

In this essential guide, Alberto Rocco reveals how artificial intelligence (AI) can be the key to transforming businesses by driving efficiency, innovation, and creativity across teams in any sector. With a practical and inspiring approach, the book presents step-by-step strategies for implementing AI, from initial planning to pilot projects and team training, ensuring that the company is prepared for a solid and lasting digital transformation.

With extensive and successful experience as an entrepreneur and a deep understanding of practical AI applications, Rocco provides insights and examples that make the content accessible and relevant. He debunks the myth that AI "kills creativity" and shows, on the contrary, how it enhances the creative side of people, freeing them to innovate and explore new ideas.

The book is enriched with a bonus section, "How AI Stimulates People's Creativity," where Rocco addresses the positive impact of AI on the human mind and the creative process, challenging limiting views on the role of technology in modern society.

For leaders, entrepreneurs, and visionary professionals, this book is more than just a read – it's a call to action. Whether in optimizing processes, personalizing experiences, or creating impactful campaigns, AI is transforming the future of business. This guide provides the roadmap for you and your company to confidently and skillfully become part of this future.

Chapter 1 - Index

Intelligent Transformation - How AI Empowers Companies and Teams in the Digital Path

1. **Introduction: The Role of AI in the Digital Age**
   - A brief overview of AI's evolution and its relevance in today's market.
   - Context on the importance of adapting companies to the AI era.
   - Goals of the ebook: clarify how AI can directly benefit companies and employees.

2. **Why Implement AI in Your Company**
   - Direct benefits of AI for business growth.
   - How AI improves efficiency, reduces costs, and creates competitive advantages.
   - Brief case studies to illustrate benefits.

3. **Preparing Company Culture for Digital Transformation**
   - The importance of an environment that values innovation and adaptation.
   - How to engage and motivate leaders and employees in adopting AI.
   - Steps to a technology-focused organizational culture shift.

4. **Employee Empowerment: The Power of AI Knowledge**
   - Reasons to train and empower employees in AI.
   - Key training areas and essential skills (use of AI tools, analytical thinking, etc.).
   - Practical examples of AI training programs.

5. **Key Business Areas Benefiting from AI**
   - **Marketing and Sales**: Personalization, audience segmentation, and behavior analysis.
   - **Customer Service**: Chatbots, predictive support, and customer experience enhancements.

- **Operations and Logistics**: Process automation, inventory management, and supply chain optimization.
- **Human Resources**: AI-assisted recruitment, performance analysis, and talent development.
- **Finance and Accounting**: Predictive analysis, fraud detection, and report automation.

6. **Strategies for AI Implementation: From Small Steps to Major Changes**
   - How to start with pilot projects and scale them as adaptation and results progress.
   - Integrating AI with existing company operations.
   - Continuous monitoring and adjustment to maximize benefits.

7. **Conclusion: The Future of the Company with AI**
   - Recap of key points covered.
   - Reflection on the importance of a vision of ongoing innovation.
   - Call to action for companies and leaders to start their journey into digital transformation.

Chapter 1: Introduction – The Role of AI in the Digital Age

In recent years, artificial intelligence (AI) has shifted from being a futuristic promise to a present reality, transforming every market sector and redefining companies' expectations for success and competitiveness. This chapter aims to place the reader within this rapidly evolving landscape, helping them understand not only AI's direct impact on the business world but also the urgency of adapting to this new digital era.

1.1 The AI Revolution: A Brief History of Innovations and Opportunities

To begin, it is essential for the reader to understand how AI evolved to become an indispensable business tool. We can start by discussing visionary companies that, even during times of technological uncertainty, bet on AI as a competitive advantage. For example:

- **Amazon**, which from its inception was a pioneer in using recommendation algorithms, personalizing purchase suggestions based on each customer's data. Today, Amazon uses AI in nearly all its operations, from inventory control to demand forecasting and customer service.
- **Tesla**, which revolutionized the automotive sector with the development of autonomous vehicles based on AI, challenging traditional mobility concepts and redefining what it means to own a car.

These companies have set standards of excellence in innovation and, at the same time, highlighted the difference between companies that embrace AI and those that resist change.

1.2 Statistics on AI Growth in the Business World

To provide a more concrete view, we include updated data showing how companies that have adopted AI stand out:

- According to research by McKinsey & Company, companies that invest in AI increase productivity by up to 40%.
- Studies show that 70% of high-growth companies use at least one AI tool in operations such as marketing, customer service, or supply chain management.
- Organizations that have implemented comprehensive AI solutions report an average 50% increase in operational efficiency.

These statistics are more than just numbers; they reflect AI's real and measurable impact. They show that by adopting AI, companies are not merely following a trend but establishing a new standard of efficiency and competitiveness.

1.3 A Comparison: Companies with AI vs. Companies Without AI

This point offers a more detailed analysis of the fundamental differences between companies that embrace AI and those that lag behind.

- **Companies that adopt AI**: These companies exhibit agility in decision-making, due to real-time data and predictive analytics. They provide personalized customer experiences,

which fosters greater loyalty, and can quickly identify innovation opportunities.
- **Companies that resist AI**: On the other hand, companies that avoid AI face challenges like a limited view of the customer, manual and inefficient operational processes, and often an insufficient pace of innovation to compete.

It's worth noting that companies without AI become more vulnerable to market fluctuations, often missing growth opportunities due to a lack of insights and agility.

1.4 Practical Example: Case Study of "Supermarket+"

Imagine the fictional company Supermarket+, a medium-sized supermarket chain operating in several cities, which for many years was successful but recently began facing competition and efficiency problems.

The Problem: Supermarket+ began noticing a decline in sales and customer engagement. Its logistics operations were overloaded, with inventories often misaligned and orders delayed, resulting in empty shelves or excess products that weren't sold in time.

The AI Solution: Realizing the need for change, Supermarket+ decided to implement AI in two main areas: logistics and customer service.

1. **AI in Logistics**: The company adopted an AI platform for demand forecasting, analyzing past sales data, seasonality, and even weather data. With this solution, they began predicting which products would be in higher demand each week, avoiding surpluses and reducing perishable product losses.
2. **AI in Customer Service**: The supermarket chain also implemented an intelligent chatbot that automatically responds to frequent customer questions about product availability, store hours, and even recipes. This not only improved service but also allowed the team to focus on more complex tasks and interactions that require a personal approach.

Results: In a short time, Supermarket+ experienced significant improvement. Sales increased due to more efficient stock management, and customer satisfaction rose after implementing the chatbot, which made service faster and more accessible.

1.5 The Current Context and the Future of AI

To conclude this chapter, we contextualize the reader within the artificial intelligence and digital transformation landscape, highlighting the rapid pace of technology growth and its increasing influence on business practices. At this point, it is essential for the reader to understand that AI is not a passing trend but a fundamental pillar for the survival and sustainable development of companies in any sector.

The Future of AI in Business: Growth and Integration

Today, expert predictions and technological advancements point to a future in which AI will be deeply integrated into virtually every business area, from customer service to financial management and product development. Market studies indicate that in the coming years, companies applying AI will have a decisive competitive advantage, increasing their capacity to innovate, optimize processes, and respond more quickly to customer and market demands.

To prepare the reader for this journey, we emphasize that AI is a constantly evolving technology that requires a continuous commitment to learning and adaptation. The companies that stand out are not necessarily those that adopt AI broadly and immediately but those that view digital transformation as a journey of continuous progress. This approach allows for a more organic and effective AI integration, adjusting strategies as market needs evolve.

Digital Transformation: A Journey, Not a Destination

Another crucial point is understanding that digital transformation, driven by AI, has no endpoint. Unlike other business initiatives with well-defined start and finish points, AI integration is a journey of continuous improvement. As new tools and methods emerge, companies need to evolve their strategies, investing in training and innovation. This process of constant adaptation is what allows companies not only to survive but to thrive in a market marked by rapid and unpredictable changes.

Preparation for the Next Steps

At the end of this chapter, the reader is prepared for an in-depth dive into the following chapters, where they will learn to use AI in a practical and strategic way within their company. The ways to empower the team, adapt processes, and implement technologies that make a real difference will be discussed. More than technical instructions, these chapters offer a growth-oriented view for sustainable and long-term success, putting the reader in control of a digital transformation that is not only innovative but essential.

With this, we conclude this powerful introduction, inviting the reader on a journey of discovery and innovation. In the upcoming chapters, they will have the knowledge needed to transform their company, using AI not only to meet current challenges but also to build a future of opportunities and advancements.

Chapter 2

Why Implement AI in Your Company

This chapter dives into the core question: why is artificial intelligence such a strategic and essential investment for companies? Here, the reader will understand that AI is not just a technological innovation but a transformation catalyst capable of redefining processes, increasing efficiency, and driving sustainable growth. We'll explore how AI can transform each sector of a company, highlighting the tangible benefits it offers modern businesses.

2.1 Key Benefits of AI for Modern Companies

To understand the broad impact of AI, it is essential to explore the main benefits it offers, always with a practical view and measurable results.

1. **Increased Productivity**:
   AI allows repetitive and time-consuming tasks to be automated, freeing employees to focus on more strategic and creative activities. This boosts productivity without necessarily increasing the workforce.

2. **Data-Driven Decisions**:
   With the ability to analyze large amounts of data in real time, AI generates insights that enable more precise and agile decisions. Rather than basing strategies on assumptions, managers can rely on concrete data, improving operational efficiency.

3. **Enhanced Customer Service**:
   AI enables a personalized customer experience, from product suggestions to faster and more efficient support. An AI system can "know" customers, understanding their preferences and proactively responding to their questions.

4. **Reduced Operational Costs**:
   AI-driven automation reduces errors and the need for rework,

minimizing costs. In complex processes, such as production and supply chain, AI helps optimize flow, making operations more economical.

5. **Innovation and Competitiveness**:
Companies using AI are seen as innovative and competitive, attracting more clients and business partners. Implementing AI not only positions the company ahead of the market but also increases its resilience to changes.

2.2 How AI Impacts Different Sectors of a Company

To show how AI can bring improvements across the organization, we describe how it applies to key company sectors, exemplifying its functionalities and results.

- **Marketing and Sales**:
  In marketing, AI can analyze customer behavior, precisely segment them, and offer personalized campaigns. Imagine an AI that, by analyzing purchasing preferences, recommends specific products to each customer, greatly increasing conversion rates. In sales, AI tools can prioritize leads, helping the team focus on potential clients more likely to make a purchase.

- **Customer Service**:
  AI enables chatbots and virtual assistants to provide 24/7 support, answering common questions and guiding clients through the purchase process. In addition to reducing the workload for the team, it enhances the customer experience with instant responses. A chatbot trained with a bank of responses can serve customers quickly and accurately, improving first-contact resolution rates.

- **Human Resources**:
  In recruitment, AI helps select candidates whose profiles align best with the company's needs, reducing hiring time and costs. In talent management, AI can analyze performance data and suggest personalized development plans for each employee, maximizing engagement and productivity.

- **Operations and Logistics**:
  AI tools assist in inventory management, optimizing delivery routes, and demand forecasting. A company that implements AI in logistics reduces waste, manages stock efficiently, and minimizes delays. With AI, it's possible to anticipate demand peaks, avoiding stockouts during high-demand periods and reducing excess inventory during slow periods.

- **Finance**:
  In finance, AI aids in risk analysis, report automation, and fraud detection. For example, AI algorithms monitor financial transactions in real time, identifying suspicious patterns and triggering preventive alerts to minimize fraud. This active monitoring improves security and protects the company from losses.

2.3 AI: A Transformative Tool and Not Just a Trend

To truly understand AI as a long-term investment, we must emphasize that it's not merely a passing fad but a transformative resource that redefines success in the market. While trends come and go, AI is quickly becoming a standard, especially in companies seeking longevity and relevance.

- **The Evolution of Business Models**:
  AI is restructuring entire sectors. Companies like Uber and Airbnb, which operate with AI-driven business models, are redefining traditional industries. This kind of transformation shows that AI not only assists operations but has the potential to reshape a company's business model.

- **The Importance of Getting Ahead**:
  The sooner a company adopts AI, the more quickly it develops a competitive advantage. In increasingly fast-paced markets, early implementation can make the difference between leading the sector and falling behind.

- **AI as a Continuous Growth Agent**:
  AI enables companies to constantly reinvent themselves. Instead of being limited to a single function or sector, it can evolve, adapt, and integrate into new processes as

opportunities and challenges arise. This flexibility is essential for a company that wants to keep pace with market changes.

2.4 Practical Example: The Impact of AI Assistants in Customer Service

To illustrate the direct impact of an AI assistant, let's consider the case of a fictional company, Atend+, specializing in electronic equipment.

Initial Scenario:
Atend+ offered customer support exclusively via phone and email, with wait times frequently exceeding 10 minutes. Customers were dissatisfied, and the volume of calls made it difficult to resolve issues quickly.

The AI Solution:
The company decided to implement an AI chatbot with a comprehensive response database and the ability to learn from each interaction. The chatbot was set up to answer frequently asked questions, such as information on products, return policies, and usage instructions.

Results:
After implementation, the average wait time dropped to less than a minute, and the chatbot was able to resolve about 70% of inquiries without human intervention. This not only reduced operational costs but also freed the team to focus on more complex issues and service improvements. Customer satisfaction increased significantly, and positive feedback translated into greater customer loyalty.

2.5 Conclusion: AI as the Foundation of a New Business Era

This chapter concludes with an essential reflection on artificial intelligence as a strategic pillar for any company seeking not only to survive but thrive in an increasingly dynamic and demanding market. AI is not just a tool for process improvement; it represents a paradigm shift that redefines what it means to be a modern company, agile and focused on customer needs.

From the examples and insights presented, the reader should now understand that AI offers more than operational optimization. It empowers companies to predict demand, quickly adapt to market changes, and meet ever-increasing customer expectations. By automating repetitive tasks and freeing the team to handle more valuable roles, AI also contributes to building a more innovative and growth-oriented organizational culture.

Implementing AI is a transformative step and a decision that resonates through all aspects of the company's operations and image. Beyond boosting productivity, AI strengthens the company's market position, building a brand synonymous with innovation, efficiency, and personalized service. By adopting AI, the company is not just following a technological trend but strategically positioning itself for the future.

A New Reality for Business Competitiveness

From this point on, the reader should realize that AI is not just an option or a luxury reserved for tech companies. In today's reality, it is a vital necessity to ensure competitiveness and sustainability. Companies that neglect this transformation risk becoming obsolete, while those that invest in AI place themselves at the forefront of the market, with unparalleled resilience to face future challenges.

Finally, this is just the first step in a journey toward digital transformation. AI is the key to opening doors to a future where innovation and efficiency go hand in hand, enabling companies to exceed current limits and create value in previously unimaginable ways. As we move on to the following chapters, the reader will not only learn to understand AI but to implement it strategically and effectively, taking their company to a new level of success and relevance in the modern market.

Chapter 3

Preparing Company Culture for Digital Transformation

This chapter explores an essential dimension of digital transformation: organizational culture. For artificial intelligence to have a truly positive and sustainable impact, the entire company—from top leadership to each employee—must be aligned and committed to this change. When AI is introduced into an organization without proper preparation, resistance, distrust, and fear are common, especially among employees who view technology as a threat.

Transforming company culture is a process that requires sensitivity, strategic vision, and a step-by-step approach that involves everyone. Below, we detail how to overcome these challenges and build a culture that embraces AI as a powerful ally.

3.1 Common Challenges in Introducing AI: Overcoming Barriers and Fears

Before outlining the cultural transformation plan, it is essential to understand the obstacles that often arise when new technology like AI is introduced. Some common barriers include:

- **Resistance to Change**: Many employees may feel comfortable with current methods and processes. The introduction of AI can be seen as disruptive, leading some to instinctively oppose any change.
- **Fear of Job Replacement**: A frequent concern is the possibility that AI will eliminate roles, especially those involving repetitive and manual tasks. This fear can generate anxiety and resistance, hindering technology acceptance.
- **Lack of Knowledge about AI**: In many organizations, employees are unfamiliar with AI's potential or limitations. Without adequate understanding, AI may be viewed as a complex and intimidating "black box."

- **Distrust in AI's Effectiveness**: In some teams, there may be skepticism about AI's real value, especially if the technology has not yet been successfully applied within the company.

These challenges are natural in any transformation, and addressing them with transparency and empathy is fundamental to laying the groundwork for effective AI adoption.

3.2 Strategy to Foster an Open and Receptive Culture for AI

To create an environment where AI is well-received, a structured plan involving all levels of the company is necessary, beginning with leadership and extending to each employee. Here is a step-by-step strategy to promote this culture of acceptance:

- **Step 1: Education and Awareness**
  The first step to integrating AI is to educate the team. It's important to organize awareness sessions explaining what AI is, how it works, and its real benefits. These sessions should demystify the technology, showing that it is not a threat but a tool to facilitate work.
    - **Practical Tips**: Organize seminars, invite AI experts for talks, and share informational materials that clarify myths about AI.
- **Step 2: Engaging Leadership and Aligning Expectations**
  For the company culture to be transformed, leadership must be fully aligned and engaged. Leaders are the primary influencers of organizational behavior, so it's essential that they are the first to believe in and support digital transformation.
    - **Practical Tips**: Organize specific meetings for leaders to discuss AI benefits, expected results, and the impact on the company. Ensure they are prepared to lead by example.
- **Step 3: Transparent and Continuous Communication**
  To reduce fear and resistance, communication about AI should be ongoing, clear, and honest. Employees need to know what to expect, which areas will be impacted, and the benefits for both them and the company.

- **Practical Tips**: Use newsletters, internal announcements, and frequent meetings to inform employees about AI implementation progress and next steps.
- **Step 4: Establish Training and Reskilling Programs**
  To help employees see AI as an opportunity rather than a threat, provide training programs to help them acquire new skills and familiarize themselves with AI tools. This not only boosts team confidence but also improves implementation effectiveness.
  - **Practical Tips**: Develop training programs to teach employees how to work with AI and empower them with new skills that will be useful in a digitalized environment.
- **Step 5: Celebrate Small Wins and Recognize Team Efforts**
  Encouraging and rewarding achievements along the journey is an effective way to keep morale high and strengthen adherence to the new culture. At each successful step, celebrate the team's adaptation and AI's positive impact.
  - **Practical Tips**: Use meetings to highlight progress, share positive customer feedback, and publicly recognize the team's efforts to adapt.

3.3 Practical Example: The AI Implementation Journey of a Medium-Sized Company's CEO

To illustrate how cultural change can be implemented in a structured and effective way, let's follow the transformation journey of a fictional company, InnovTech, a medium-sized firm that decided to adopt AI to optimize operations and enhance customer experience.

Initial Scenario:
InnovTech operated with traditional methods, and its team had little or no experience with AI. When presenting the AI adoption plan, CEO Carlos Mendes noticed a mix of curiosity and apprehension among employees. It was clear to him that before implementing the technology, it would be necessary to prepare the team for this change.

- **Action 1: Immersive AI Workshop for Leadership**
  Carlos organized a two-day immersive workshop for

department leaders. At this event, he brought in an AI specialist to cover the basics, debunk myths, and present case studies on how AI can be an ally. This gathering not only clarified doubts but generated enthusiasm among leaders, who were now ready to become advocates for the transformation.

- **Action 2: Practical Training Sessions and Group Activities**
  To ease AI acceptance among all employees, InnovTech offered practical training sessions and group activities. In these sessions, employees were encouraged to try out simple AI tools, like chatbot assistants, and share their impressions. Activities included simulations where employees "competed" with the chatbot to respond faster, highlighting AI's role as support rather than a replacement.

- **Action 3: Creation of an Open Communication Channel**
  Carlos launched an internal communication channel called "InnovTech Talks," where employees could ask questions and share experiences about the new phase of transformation. This channel was crucial for quickly clarifying doubts and resolving concerns, helping everyone feel more confident about the process.

- **Action 4: Celebrating Initial Achievements**
  A few months later, InnovTech implemented AI in customer support triage and administrative process automation. Upon seeing improvements, Carlos called a general meeting to share initial results, thank the team for their commitment, and recognize the leaders who drove the transformation. This acknowledgment generated a sense of accomplishment and motivation for the next steps.

3.4 The Path to a Continuous Transformation Culture

To close this chapter, we emphasize that cultural transformation is the true foundation for AI's success in any organization. AI adoption cannot be seen as a one-time event or an isolated initiative; it needs to be integrated into the essence of the company, which requires a continuous process of adaptation, learning, and evolution.

Once the company culture is open to AI, it's necessary to nurture this mindset of innovation and continuous improvement. This means encouraging the team to constantly seek knowledge, try new tools, and find new ways to use AI to solve challenges and enhance customer experience. Each employee should feel like a part of the transformation, understanding that their role is not replaced but expanded by AI and that this journey's success depends on both technology and the engagement and evolution of the people involved.

Innovation Culture as a Competitive Advantage

Cultivating a culture of continuous transformation creates a powerful competitive advantage. In an increasingly agile market, a company that encourages its team to adapt quickly and innovate constantly is prepared not only to respond to changes but to lead transformations in its sector. This is the essence of an innovation culture: an environment where AI is not seen as a substitute but as an amplifier of human talent, and where employees become protagonists in the digital journey.

Next Steps in the Digital Journey: From Culture to Action

With this cultural foundation established, the company is ready for a new chapter in its digital transformation journey. In the following chapters, we will explore how to apply AI to daily processes in a practical and strategic way, maximizing its value across all operations. The reader will learn to create training programs for the entire team, identify areas with the greatest transformation potential, and implement AI in ways that not only improve efficiency but also inspire innovation and growth throughout the organization.

Adapting to AI is more than a commitment to technology; it's a commitment to the future. The path forward is one of exploration, learning, and continuous expansion. This journey will ensure that the company not only follows market trends but positions itself as a leader, making AI an essential tool for achieving ambitious goals, always with an eye on human development and the positive impact technology can have on people's lives and the workplace.

This conclusion offers the reader an inspiring glimpse of what's to come, preparing them to turn this innovative culture into practical actions, consolidating a future where AI and human capital work together to build a more resilient, efficient, and growth-oriented business.

Chapter 4

Empowering Employees - The Power of AI Knowledge

In this chapter, readers will find a practical guide to training employees in the use of AI, transforming theory into concrete action. Training is the essential link to making artificial intelligence not just a technology present in the company but an active tool understood and utilized by everyone. When employees master the use of AI, it becomes part of the daily routine, generating productivity gains and valuable insights for the business.

4.1 Essential Knowledge for Operating with AI Tools

To effectively use AI, employees need knowledge in two main areas: technical skills and analytical abilities. These skills vary depending on role and level of responsibility, but all employees, regardless of position, can benefit from these fundamentals.

- **Basic Technical Skills**:
  Employees should be familiar with AI tools and know how to apply them in their routines. For operational roles, understanding automation and intuitive interfaces, like chatbots and digital assistants, is useful. For leadership and strategic roles, knowledge of analytical tools such as predictive analysis and data visualization is essential.

- **Data Analysis and Interpretation**:
  The ability to interpret data is one of the most valued skills in an AI-driven environment. Trained employees can identify patterns, predict trends, and better understand customer behavior. This skill is crucial for transforming AI-collected data into informed and strategic decisions.

- **Critical Thinking and Problem Solving**:
  AI provides information and recommendations, but the final decision still rests with humans. Training employees to question, analyze, and validate AI-generated insights ensures

that the team uses AI recommendations as support for sound decisions, rather than definitive answers.

4.2 Training Methods to Equip the Team in AI

To ease adaptation to AI, the company should invest in comprehensive and adaptable training programs. Here are some effective approaches:

- **Practical Workshops**:
  Workshops offer an immersive, hands-on experience where employees can explore and apply AI in real situations. During workshops, simulations and case studies can help the team safely and securely use AI tools.
    - **Example**: A predictive analysis workshop for the marketing team could teach them how to interpret customer behavior data and predict buying trends.
- **E-learning Modules and Continuous Training**:
  E-learning enables employees to access training content at their own pace. Online courses can be divided into modules, covering everything from AI basics to specific software operations, such as natural language processing tools or recommendation algorithms.
    - **Example**: Create a modular e-learning program that covers AI fundamentals to specific software use for predictive analysis. Each employee can complete the modules best suited to their role.
- **Mentoring and Interdepartmental Training Sessions**:
  To reinforce learning, mentoring sessions where more experienced employees guide their colleagues in their initial AI experiences are beneficial. Mentoring fosters a supportive environment and knowledge sharing, making learning more organic and effective.
    - **Example**: IT team members with AI experience can lead training sessions with employees from other departments, such as sales and finance, helping them understand AI applications in their specific areas.
- **Soft Skills and Human Skills Development**:
  Beyond technical skills, AI training requires developing

interpersonal skills. Soft skills, like communication, adaptability, and collaboration, are essential for successful AI implementation, ensuring technology is integrated harmoniously and productively.

4.3 The Importance of Continuous Training

AI-driven digital transformation is a dynamic and evolving process. New tools, methods, and insights continually emerge, and a company that wants to stay competitive must foster a culture of constant learning. Training is not a one-time event but a long-term investment with lasting returns.

Keeping employees up to date means not only training them in current technology but also preparing them for future innovations. This process creates a work environment that values personal and professional growth, helping employees see AI not as a passing novelty but as an essential part of their growth and the company's success.

- **Incentives for Continuous Growth**:
  To encourage ongoing learning, the company can offer rewards and recognition to those who complete advanced training or demonstrate proficiency with AI tools. This type of incentive helps create a culture of knowledge appreciation and motivates employees to improve their skills.

4.4 Practical Example: Simulation of an Internal AI Training Program

To illustrate the impact of structured AI training, let's imagine the training program implemented by the fictional company DataGrow, a medium-sized digital marketing company.

Initial Scenario:
DataGrow recognized that to stand out in the market, it needed to train its team to use AI in marketing campaigns. The CEO identified that both the marketing and IT teams could benefit from AI learning, especially to enhance data analysis and customer segmentation.

The Training Program: A Modular Approach
The program was structured into three main modules with different levels of complexity:

- **Module 1: AI Fundamentals**
  All employees participated in this initial module, which covered the basics of AI, myths and truths, and the technology's impact on digital marketing. This module included a practical workshop where the team learned to use a simple predictive analysis tool to forecast customer behavior trends.

- **Module 2: AI Tools Applied to Marketing**
  Marketing employees attended this intermediate module, which introduced specific AI tools for data analysis and customer segmentation. Each marketing team member began using tools like social media sentiment analysis and recommendation algorithms to improve campaign personalization.

- **Module 3: Advanced Predictive Analysis**
  This module was offered to the IT team and marketing managers, focusing on advanced predictive analysis concepts, including how to interpret machine learning models and generate strategic insights. The module included creating an AI application project, where managers developed a data-driven campaign supervised by expert mentors.

Results:
After completing the program, DataGrow saw a significant increase in campaign efficiency, with a higher return on marketing investment. Trained employees began using AI to quickly analyze large volumes of data, identifying insights that previously took days to discover manually. This resulted in a more confident team and a workplace where innovation is valued and encouraged.

4.5 Conclusion of Chapter 4: Knowledge as a Driver of Transformation

To conclude this chapter, it is crucial to highlight that AI training is not merely a necessary step for implementing new technologies; it is the driving force that can transform the company from within. By investing in developing employee skills, the company is not only updating its human capital but building a solid and sustainable foundation for future challenges and opportunities. Each trained employee is a multiplier of potential, ready to apply AI with confidence, innovation, and responsibility.

Preparing for the Future: An Aligned and Engaged Team

By strengthening AI knowledge at all organizational levels—from operations to leadership—the company positions itself as an entity that not only understands the present but is also prepared to shape the future. This alignment of skills and vision among all employees creates synergy, where every team member understands their role and impact in digital transformation. AI ceases to be seen as something distant or complex and becomes a practical and valuable tool accessible and useful to every sector of the company.

Shared Knowledge as a Foundation for Growth and Innovation

When AI knowledge is disseminated and shared, it becomes a lever for collective innovation. Each employee begins to see AI as an extension of their abilities, using it to explore new ideas, solve complex problems, and propose more effective solutions. This foundation of shared knowledge allows AI to be used strategically, focusing not just on automating tasks but on identifying new growth opportunities, optimizing processes, and enhancing the customer experience.

A New Level of Competitiveness and Efficiency

With a well-trained and motivated team, the company is ready to fully explore the opportunities offered by AI. The organization reaches a new level of competitiveness, where efficiency is not just a goal but a natural outcome of a workplace where technology and human talent complement each other. The ability to continuously innovate, based on analytical insights and a qualified team, becomes a market differentiator that positions the company ahead of its competitors.

Next Steps: Turning Training into Practical Action

In the following chapters, readers will learn how to turn this training into practical actions, applying the knowledge gained to specific projects and key sectors. Each application of AI becomes more strategic and integrated into daily operations, making technology a natural and essential component of the company's everyday functions. This next stage of the digital journey ensures that AI is not just an occasional tool but a vital element for achieving growth, adaptability, and operational excellence that define success in the modern era.

This conclusion reinforces that training is more than learning—it is a continuous investment in the company's future, a commitment to human and technological development, and the foundation for building an organization truly innovative and prepared to thrive in the age of artificial intelligence.

Chapter 5

Key Business Areas that Benefit from AI

In this chapter, we explore the strategic areas of a business where artificial intelligence has the potential to add significant value. To help readers visualize AI's practical impact in each sector, each section is guided by specific examples and applicable tools, demonstrating how AI can transform operations and enhance performance across various KPIs (key performance indicators).

5.1 Marketing and Sales: AI as an Ally in Personalization and Efficiency

In marketing and sales, AI is a valuable resource that enables campaign personalization, predictive behavior analysis, and a better understanding of the target audience. Using machine learning algorithms, AI processes large amounts of data to identify consumer behavior patterns, predict trends, and adjust strategies in real time.

Specific Tools and Applications:

- **Sentiment Analysis and Customer Feedback**: AI-based sentiment analysis software allows companies to monitor customer opinions on social media, identifying satisfaction patterns in real time.
- **Recommendation Systems**: AI algorithms can recommend personalized products or services based on customer preferences and purchase history.
- **Predictive Purchasing Analysis**: AI tools can predict consumer preferences and future behaviors, helping sales teams anticipate demand and adjust inventory.

Practical Example: A fictional online retail company, ShopSmart, implemented AI to personalize email marketing campaigns based on each customer's purchase and browsing history. Using a recommendation system, the emails are personalized with products likely to interest the customer. As a result, open and click-through rates increased by 25%, and email sales grew by 30%, strengthening customer loyalty and improving conversion metrics.

5.2 Customer Service: AI in Creating Fast and Satisfying Experiences

Customer service is one of the areas where AI directly impacts the customer experience. With chatbots, virtual assistants, and automated service, AI improves support efficiency and offers quick, accurate responses, creating a more satisfying customer experience.

Specific Tools and Applications:

- **Chatbots**: AI software that automatically responds to the most common customer questions, reducing wait time and freeing up the team to focus on more complex issues.
- **Virtual Assistants with Natural Language Processing (NLP)**: Tools that use NLP to interpret and respond to complex questions, simulating human interactions and providing advanced support.
- **Sentiment Analysis in Support Calls**: AI can detect the customer's emotional tone during a call or text message, adjusting support and prioritizing urgent cases.

Practical Example: TechAssist, a company specializing in electronics, implemented an AI chatbot to handle frequent questions about its products and return policies. The chatbot resolves 70% of customer inquiries without human intervention, reducing response time from 10 minutes to less than 1 minute. As a result, the company saw a 40% increase in customer satisfaction and a significant reduction in customer service operational costs.

5.3 Human Resources: AI in Recruitment and Talent Management

In human resources, AI offers solutions to improve recruitment, performance analysis, and talent retention. With AI tools, it's possible to evaluate candidates more objectively, predict cultural fit, and identify employees with the highest development potential.

Specific Tools and Applications:

- **Resume Analysis and Automated Filters**: AI tools that analyze resumes en masse, quickly identifying candidates who meet the criteria.
- **Data-Based Performance Analysis**: AI algorithms can assess employee performance based on productivity, engagement, and skills metrics.
- **Retention Analysis and Turnover Prevention**: AI can identify behavior patterns indicating a risk of turnover and propose retention strategies.

Practical Example: At TalentBoost, a consulting company, the HR team implemented AI to optimize the recruitment process. AI quickly analyzes large volumes of resumes, using filters to find candidates most aligned with the company's needs. Additionally, the tool provides insights on retention probability based on past interviews and cultural assessments. This approach reduced the time to fill positions by 50% and significantly improved new hires' cultural fit.

5.4 Operations and Logistics: AI for Optimization and Efficiency

In operations and logistics, AI offers invaluable value for optimizing routes, managing inventories, and predicting demand. These improvements ensure an efficient product flow, enabling the company to meet demand without interruptions, reduce waste, and maximize efficiency.

Specific Tools and Applications:

- **Route Planning with AI**: Tools that use real-time data to plan more efficient delivery routes, reducing transportation time and fuel consumption.
- **Inventory Management and Demand Forecasting**: AI algorithms that analyze past sales data, seasonality, and trends to predict future demand and adjust stock levels.
- **Warehouse Automation**: AI tools that coordinate product movement and organize stock intelligently.

Practical Example: FastSupply, a logistics company, implemented AI to improve its route and inventory management system. AI analyzes real-time traffic data, optimizing delivery routes to reduce transport time by 20%. Additionally, with accurate demand forecasting, the company reduced excess inventory by 30%, saving on storage costs and increasing logistical efficiency.

5.5 Finance and Accounting: AI for Financial Analysis and Risk Management

In finance, AI plays a crucial role in automating accounting processes, analyzing financial data, and managing risks. AI can identify patterns in financial data, assist in fraud detection, and generate insights that help the company make safer, data-driven financial decisions.

Specific Tools and Applications:

- **Accounting Process Automation**: AI tools that automate accounting tasks, such as expense classification, account reconciliation, and financial reporting.
- **Risk Analysis and Fraud Detection**: AI monitors transactions in real time, identifying suspicious patterns and sending preventive alerts.
- **Financial Forecasting and Scenario Analysis**: AI tools that project future cash flows and analyze different financial scenarios to support strategic decision-making.

Practical Example: FinanceTech, a financial services company, implemented AI to monitor transactions and detect fraud in real time. Using algorithms that identify suspicious activity, the company reduced fraud losses by 40%. Additionally, AI-driven financial forecasting tools enabled the finance department to project cash flows and adjust the budget with precision, enhancing security and operational reliability.

Conclusion of Chapter 5: AI as a Pillar for an Innovative and Efficient Company

Throughout this chapter, we demonstrated how artificial intelligence can be the foundation that transforms every area of a company, from marketing to finance, in a profound and comprehensive way. AI provides a new dimension of efficiency, insight, and responsiveness that was previously unimaginable, allowing each sector to become more productive, agile, and innovative. With AI tools applied in marketing, customer service, human resources, operations, and finance, the company not only becomes more competitive but also establishes a solid foundation for continuous and sustainable growth.

Positioning the Company at a New Level of Competitiveness

Strategic AI adoption across key areas enables the company to differentiate itself from competitors and position itself as a high-performance organization. AI empowers the company to deeply understand its customers, optimize resources, reduce costs, and innovate continuously. This level of competitiveness places the organization ahead of market trends, where it not only responds to changes but anticipates opportunities and sets new standards of efficiency and quality.

Building a Culture of Data-Driven Decisions

Integrating AI brings a cultural shift where decisions are based on robust data and analyses, rather than assumptions or intuition. This data-driven approach creates a more aligned work environment, where all employees, from operational to leadership levels, share a strategically results-oriented vision. The company moves beyond operating based on past experiences and builds its future with clarity and confidence, guided by the insights AI provides.

Next Steps: Applying AI in a Strategic and Integrated Way

In the following chapters, readers will learn how to turn this vision into practical actions, applying AI in daily operations and creating synergy between technology and operations. The journey continues with strategies for implementing AI in an integrated way, ensuring technology becomes part of the company's DNA, strengthening the culture of innovation and enabling each department to work at its maximum potential. This journey towards a more intelligent, data-driven company not only ensures survival in a constantly changing market but allows the organization to thrive and lead the path of innovation, establishing itself as a reference in its sector.

AI as the Engine of Continuous Transformation

As the company advances on this journey, AI will not just be a tool but the engine of continuous transformation. This evolution will allow the company to constantly explore new performance frontiers, establishing a growth cycle where innovation and technology mutually reinforce each other. This chapter closes an initial cycle of understanding the benefits of AI across various areas, but opens the door to strategic implementation that will solidify the company as an agile organization, capable of reinventing itself and reaching new heights of excellence.

The next step is to integrate this powerful technology cohesively into every operation, every decision, and every interaction, making AI a fundamental part of the company's long-term success and the construction of a future with unlimited opportunities.

Chapter 6

Strategies for AI Implementation

This chapter serves as a practical guide for implementing AI in the company, dividing the process into clear, actionable steps. AI implementation should be well-planned, prioritizing high-impact areas where technology can deliver measurable and immediate results. By following these strategies, the company can explore AI's potential with safety and control, ensuring a gradual and effective transition to digital transformation.

6.1 Pilot Projects: Starting Small to Validate Impact

Implementing AI across the entire company at once can be challenging, risky, and costly. Therefore, starting with pilot projects is a recommended practice to test AI effectiveness in specific areas before expanding its use. Pilot projects are small-scale initiatives applied to a single sector or process to assess the technology's impact and identify potential challenges and opportunities.

Advantages of Pilot Projects:

- **Controlled Risk**: Pilot projects allow testing AI in a controlled environment, reducing financial and operational risks.
- **Impact Evaluation**: With a pilot, the company can monitor and measure AI's impact, adjusting the approach based on initial results.
- **Feedback for Improvement**: These projects provide valuable feedback from employees and managers, enabling improvements before a large-scale rollout.

Pilot Project Example: Imagine a company that wants to implement AI in customer service. The pilot project might involve installing a chatbot in a specific support channel, like chat support, to answer frequently asked questions. During the pilot, the company would monitor the number of interactions handled by the chatbot, response time, and customer satisfaction, comparing these results to traditional service methods. With the data and feedback obtained, the company can decide whether to expand chatbot use to other customer service areas.

6.2 Evaluating AI Vendors and Ensuring Quality

Choosing reliable, high-quality AI vendors is essential for successful implementation. There are numerous AI solution providers on the market, but the choice should consider factors beyond cost. To ensure the AI solution meets the company's specific needs, carefully evaluate vendors and ensure the quality of the solutions offered.

Criteria for Evaluating AI Vendors:

- **Industry Experience**: Check if the vendor has experience serving companies in the same industry, indicating an understanding of specific needs and challenges.
- **Support and Training**: Choose vendors that offer technical support and team training, ensuring a smoother implementation and adaptation.
- **Customization Capability**: AI solutions need to be adaptable to the company's operations. Assess whether the vendor allows customizations or integrations that enhance the fit of AI in the work environment.
- **Security and Compliance**: AI solutions must meet security and regulatory compliance requirements, especially in sensitive sectors like finance and healthcare.

Quality Assurance: The quality of implemented AI is crucial for its effectiveness. Before committing, ask the vendor to provide a practical demonstration of the technology. Additionally, seek customer reviews to ensure the performance and support meet expectations.

6.3 Measuring Success and Return on Investment (ROI) of AI Implementations

AI implementation should generate measurable value for the business. To evaluate an AI project's success, it's essential to define key performance indicators (KPIs) and calculate the return on investment (ROI). These indicators not only monitor AI progress but also help adjust and improve implementation over time.

Defining KPIs for AI Implementations:

- **Cost Reduction**: In areas where AI automates manual processes, KPIs can include reductions in staffing costs or time savings.
- **Improvement in Customer Experience**: In customer service, KPIs such as average response time and customer satisfaction index help measure AI's impact.
- **Productivity Increase**: In operations and logistics, productivity can be evaluated by delivery speed and accuracy or resource optimization.

Calculating AI ROI: To calculate ROI, subtract the total project cost (including software investment, training, and maintenance) from the benefits generated, such as cost reductions and revenue increases. Divide the result by the total cost and multiply by 100 to obtain the ROI percentage.

- **Example**: If an AI chatbot in customer service reduces average service time by 30% and generates annual savings of $100,000, with a total implementation cost of $50,000, the ROI would be:
  ROI = (100,000−50,000)/50,000×100=100%
  (100,000−50,000)/50,000×100=100%

6.4 Practical Example: Implementation Roadmap for a Pilot Project

To illustrate the AI implementation process, let's imagine an implementation roadmap for a pilot project in the customer service area of a fictional company, ServiceCo.

Phase 1: Initial Planning

1. **Problem Identification and Goal Setting**: ServiceCo identifies that the average customer response time is long and sets a goal to reduce response time by 20% with AI.
2. **Selecting the AI Tool**: After evaluating vendors, the company chooses a chatbot capable of answering common questions and redirecting complex issues to human agents.

3. **Defining KPIs**: ServiceCo defines KPIs such as average response time, customer satisfaction index, and volume of automated interactions.

Phase 2: Implementation and Testing

1. **Chatbot Setup**: The company implements the chatbot in a specific channel, such as website chat support.
2. **Team Training**: The customer service team is trained to oversee the chatbot and intervene in complex cases.
3. **Controlled Launch**: The chatbot is launched for a small sample of customers, allowing the collection of initial feedback.

Phase 3: Monitoring and Analyzing Results

1. **Data Collection**: Over the first three months, ServiceCo collects data on the chatbot's performance.
2. **Evaluating Results**: Based on the KPIs, the company finds that response time decreased by 25% and customer satisfaction increased.
3. **Expansion Decision**: Given the pilot project's success, ServiceCo decides to expand chatbot use to other customer service channels, such as social media and email.

6.5 Conclusion of Chapter 6: Implementing AI with Safety and Effectiveness

This chapter provided a practical and structured approach to implementing artificial intelligence, emphasizing the importance of starting with small steps, like pilot projects, which allow the company to test and validate technology in controlled environments. By selecting reliable vendors, defining relevant KPIs, and measuring ROI, the company not only reduces risks but also builds a solid foundation for success. This methodology ensures that AI is introduced strategically, adding measurable value and strengthening confidence in technology as a crucial resource for growth.

Strategy and Analysis: The Pillars of AI Transformation

The success of AI implementation is not just about technological innovation but also about strategic clarity and rigorous analysis at every stage. This data-driven approach enables the company to identify and resolve initial challenges, maximize results, and continually learn from each phase of implementation. By measuring

AI's impact through KPIs and ROI, the company can validate and adjust its strategies, ensuring that each implementation is both efficient and aligned with long-term goals.

Continuous Integration and Collaboration between AI and Human Capital

In the coming chapters, readers will explore how to integrate AI continuously, expanding successful pilot projects and increasing AI presence across various sectors of the organization. The journey to building a smart, data-driven company is gradual and evolutionary, with each step representing progress toward a more agile, productive, and competitive operation. As AI becomes a natural and fluid part of operations, human capital is also strengthened, with employees taking on new roles in analysis, oversight, and innovation.

A Future where AI and Human Talent Drive Success

This chapter laid the groundwork for the company to advance confidently in its digital journey. The combination of AI's precision and efficiency with the strategic vision and adaptability of employees enables the organization not only to adapt to market changes but to anticipate and lead transformation. By building a future where AI and human capital work together, the company is positioned to face new challenges and capture opportunities quickly, efficiently, and innovatively.

This grounded and collaborative approach ensures that AI is a continuous and sustainable resource, paving the way for a business that thrives and stands out, always one step ahead of market demands and trends. In the coming chapters, readers will discover how to turn these strategies into practical actions, establishing AI as an essential pillar for innovation and sustainable organizational growth.

Chapter 7

Conclusion - The Future of the Company with AI

As we conclude this journey through the realm of artificial intelligence, it's essential to emphasize that AI implementation is not just a project but a continuous journey of adaptation and evolution. AI doesn't just transform processes and operations; it redefines how companies position themselves in the market, respond to challenges, and create value. This transformative power, however, only fully materializes when the company adopts a culture of constant learning, where technological development goes hand-in-hand with employee training and innovation.

7.1 AI: A Journey of Continuous Adaptation and Learning

Adopting AI isn't merely about implementing new technologies; it's a commitment to a new way of thinking and operating. AI is constantly evolving, bringing new resources and opportunities that require a proactive stance from the company. With each new tool, the company not only enhances its processes but also grows in digital maturity and adapts to market changes with greater agility.

Leaders and employees must be willing to learn and adapt continuously. This ongoing learning enables AI to not only optimize the present but also prepare the company for the future, helping it tackle challenges with innovation and strategic vision. Companies that remain open to learning and experimentation become more resilient and better positioned to capitalize on opportunities in a rapidly changing market.

7.2 AI Implementation as a Growth Journey

Implementing AI is much more than a one-time task; it's a journey of continuous growth. From pilot projects to expansions across different areas, AI offers valuable insights that, when integrated into the company's strategy, translate into a solid competitive advantage. Throughout this journey, AI projects should be seen as building blocks for a more agile, customer-centric, and data-driven organization.

Each stage of AI implementation brings learning and generates value, whether through personalized customer interactions, process optimization, or data-driven decision-making. This journey has no end: it is a process of constant improvement that adapts to technological innovations and changing customer demands.

7.3 A 90-Day Plan to Begin AI Implementation

To help readers take their first steps in a practical and effective way, we present a 90-day action plan. This plan offers an initial roadmap to start AI implementation in the company, encouraging readers to turn the ideas presented throughout the book into concrete actions.

Days 1-30: Assessment and Planning

- **Identify Priority Areas**: Choose sectors or processes that can quickly and measurably benefit from AI, such as customer service, marketing, or logistics.
- **Set Goals and KPIs**: Establish clear objectives and performance indicators to assess AI's impact, such as cost reduction, productivity increase, or customer satisfaction improvement.
- **Research AI Vendors**: Evaluate reliable vendors that offer solutions aligned with the company's needs and goals. Consider factors such as support, customization, and security.

Days 31-60: Implementing a Pilot Project

- **Launch a Pilot Project**: Start a pilot project in a chosen area. For example, implement a customer service chatbot or a predictive analysis tool in marketing.
- **Train the Team**: Provide training for employees who will use the new technology. Ensure everyone understands how AI adds value and how it can be integrated into their workflow.
- **Monitor Performance**: Closely monitor the defined KPIs, collecting data and feedback from the team and customers to evaluate the project's effectiveness.

Days 61-90: Evaluation and Expansion

- **Evaluate Results**: Compare pilot project data with the initially established KPIs and goals. Identify what worked well and what can be adjusted.
- **Adjust and Optimize**: Based on the results analysis, make adjustments to improve the pilot project's effectiveness. Enhance training, refine processes, and adjust goals as needed.
- **Plan for Expansion**: If the pilot project is successful, develop an expansion plan for other company areas. Also, consider how the insights and learning gained can be applied to new AI projects.

This 90-day plan provides a practical and feasible foundation to start AI implementation, allowing the company to move forward in a controlled and effective manner. Each stage is a learning opportunity, preparing the team and the company for a gradual and sustainable AI integration.

7.4 Conclusion: Committing to an Innovative, AI-Driven Future

Upon completing this journey of learning and planning, the reader is now equipped with a powerful set of tools, insights, and strategies to make AI an essential pillar of their company. AI implementation does not signify the end of digital transformation but rather the beginning of a new phase, marked by continuous innovation, ongoing learning, and sustainable growth. Each successful project and lesson learned along this journey will strengthen the company, positioning it as an agile, resilient, and truly data-driven organization.

A New Stage of Growth and Adaptation

Commitment to AI opens doors for a company capable of quickly adapting to market changes and anticipating customer needs with intelligence and precision. Instead of merely reacting to market events, the company becomes proactive, guided by insights and oriented toward the future. This not only solidifies its current position but also creates new growth and differentiation opportunities in a highly competitive landscape.

Turning Knowledge into Action: A Call to Lead the Change

The call to action is now clear: it's time to turn acquired knowledge into practice. Each chapter of this book was designed to provide the reader not only with concepts but also with practical steps to drive digital transformation confidently and clearly. By implementing AI strategically and integratively, the reader will combine the power of technology with human talent, creating an organizational culture that values innovation and efficiency. This process will ensure that the company not only survives the changes of the digital age but thrives and inspires the sector with its innovations.

An Unlimited Future Full of Opportunities

Artificial intelligence offers a dynamic future filled with unlimited possibilities. By building a journey of continuous transformation, the company won't just keep up with the pace of change in the digital world but will position itself as an active force of transformation. Every step, every new implementation, and every innovation will contribute to a legacy of progress, where AI and human capital complement and empower each other.

This is the beginning of a virtuous cycle, where learning and adaptation become a constant practice. By adopting a proactive, forward-looking stance, the company will be ready to face any challenge and capitalize on all the opportunities that AI advancement provides. Thus, this journey with AI becomes much more than a business strategy—it becomes the foundation of a resilient, innovative company prepared to create lasting value in a world increasingly driven by artificial intelligence.

With this, the reader is ready to lead this transformation and make AI a decisive factor in success, efficiency, and innovation, consolidating a legacy of excellence and vision in a future filled with possibilities.

PROLOGUE

In the accelerated digital transformation landscape, many focus on the technology itself but overlook a critical aspect: preparing and empowering employees to embrace and implement these changes confidently and effectively. For AI to truly transform your business, it is essential that the team is not only familiar but genuinely skilled in the tools and principles that drive this new digital era. Only then, when the time for complete transformation arrives, will employees be ready to adopt advanced, specific AI solutions with ease, becoming active agents of this change.

With this vision in mind, we offer Darwin48, an intensive two-day program designed to prepare your team and you for the future with AI. Darwin48 is more than a Boot Camp; it's a complete immersion, a practical experience that combines innovation, impact, and applicability. Created for entrepreneurs, managers, and visionary professionals in any sector, Darwin48 covers the most advanced AI tools for business and focuses on the skills that truly make a difference.

Why Join Darwin48?

Through Darwin48, you will learn to master fundamental AI tools, including:

- **Mastering AI Tools**: From content creation with ChatGPT to image, video, and audio generation with cutting-edge technology, you and your team will be equipped with the practical skills to apply AI in multiple areas of the business.
- **Customer Attraction Strategies**: Discover how AI-driven campaigns can capture your audience's attention and expand your customer base.
- **Process Optimization**: Understand how AI can reduce costs, streamline workflows, and increase your company's efficiency.

Participation Options:

To make this experience accessible and convenient, we offer several registration options:

- **Basic Entry**: Full access to the two-day Boot Camp.
- **Complete Package**: Includes access to the event, accommodation, and meals for a worry-free experience.

Choose the option that best suits your needs and dive into this transformation journey.

Don't Get Left Behind. Join Darwin48 and Bring the Future to Your Business!

More information at illutio.biz.

This is the first step to ensuring your team and company are at the forefront of digital transformation. The future belongs to those who are prepared—take this decisive step with Alberto Rocco and Darwin48.

Bonus Chapter

How AI Stimulates Creativity in People

In the worlds of art and business, there is a recurring concern: would AI, with its automated solutions and predictive algorithms, "kill" human creativity? However, a deeper analysis reveals that AI, far from being a threat, can be a powerful ally to amplify human imagination and innovation. Creativity, by definition, is the ability to see the world from a new perspective, connect ideas, and create something unique. When used correctly, AI provides tools to expand this capacity, acting as a true "creative catalyst."

In this chapter, we explore how the mind interacts with AI and how it can unlock new ideas and creative paths. We examine practical examples and offer a psychological analysis of how AI can enrich rather than stifle the creative process.

The Nature of Creativity and the Role of AI as a Partner

Creativity is a fundamental characteristic of the human mind, fueled by curiosity, experimentation, and the ability to see beyond the obvious. When we use AI in the creative process, it enhances these innate abilities. AI provides an almost infinite amount of information, models, and inspirations that the human brain can filter, reinterpret, and use as a foundation for creating something new. Rather than replacing the creative drive, AI serves as an extension of our capabilities, helping us access resources and references that would otherwise be out of reach.

For example, using AI tools to generate visual ideas, such as settings or characters for a narrative, AI may provide initial suggestions, but it's the human mind that chooses, refines, and transforms these suggestions into something meaningful and original.

Psychology of Creativity with AI: How the Mind Interacts and Expands

To understand how AI can stimulate creativity, we need to explore how the mind processes new and complex information. Cognitive psychology suggests that creativity results from connections between areas of the brain that don't always "communicate" with each other. This process, known as "associative thinking," allows different experiences, knowledge, and ideas to come together to form something new.

AI, by providing large-scale data, models, and even simulations, expands the range of associations available to the brain. By offering suggestions based on patterns, AI doesn't replace creative judgment but offers "starting points" that the creator can reinterpret and adapt. This is the concept of "guided creative exploration," where AI presents possibilities, and the human brain selects and shapes these ideas.

Practical Example:

Imagine a designer tasked with creating a new line of home decor products. Using an AI tool, they receive countless options for color combinations, styles, and materials. Instead of starting from scratch, the designer begins with a series of visual proposals from AI. By exploring these suggestions, they can reconfigure and combine elements to create something new and original. AI presents variations they might not have considered, but the choice and adjustment process is entirely creative.

AI and the Stimulation of "Creative Flow"

One of the psychological conditions that favor creativity is the state of "flow," an experience of complete immersion in an activity where the creator feels challenged and engaged but without stress. AI can help facilitate this state by eliminating repetitive tasks and streamlining processes that often prevent creators from delving into their ideas.

Practical Example:

In developing a marketing campaign, a creative team must analyze data, identify trends, and structure impactful content. With AI's help in analyzing large volumes of consumer behavior data and even suggesting initial content structures, the team has more time to focus on creative nuances. AI handles the "preparatory tasks," allowing professionals to enter the flow more easily and explore their creativity without operational distractions.

AI as an Inspiration and "Idea Provoker"

For many artists and creators, AI offers something beyond suggestions; it provokes new interpretations and diverts attention from the obvious. Rather than being an execution tool, AI can function as an "idea provocateur" by generating possibilities that challenge creators to explore new territories.

Psychological Analysis:

Exposure to new and unconventional ideas and stimuli is known to unlock creative processes. This is especially relevant in art and innovation, where creative "insight" often arises from unexpected stimuli. AI, by generating unusual combinations, offers precisely this kind of stimulus. The brain, when confronted with these possibilities, responds with a creative response, seeking to make sense of the unexpected and connecting it to its own experience and cultural background.

Practical Example:

A writer uses an AI tool to generate visual descriptions of dystopian settings for a novel. AI suggests futuristic landscapes with surreal elements, sparking curiosity and challenging the writer to expand their concept of "dystopia." From these descriptions, the author finds inspiration to create settings and characters that defy genre conventions, exploring elements that might not have naturally emerged from their own mind.

Debunking the Myth: AI and Creative Autonomy

The idea that AI "kills" creativity often stems from a limited understanding of the human mind's creative nature. Creativity isn't defined by creation from scratch; it's the ability to build, reinterpret, and connect ideas. AI doesn't replace human vision and imagination but amplifies and offers new paths for the human mind to explore.

It's important to see AI as an extension of the creative process, something that gives the creator more resources and opportunities for expression. Rather than limiting creativity, AI allows more people in different fields and with varying levels of skill to explore their own creative potential in ways that were previously impossible.

Conclusion: AI as a Catalyst for Human Creativity

In this chapter, we have seen how AI doesn't limit creativity but expands it. By offering suggestions, handling operational tasks, and presenting alternatives, AI acts as a creative partner, allowing the human mind to access a broader range of ideas and connections. The creative process doesn't lose its essence; it gains a new dimension.

Ultimately, AI stimulates creativity by enabling people to dive into what truly matters: the exploration of ideas and the discovery of new perspectives. Creativity isn't a capability that can be erased but a force that evolves and grows, and AI is the fuel that accelerates this growth. By recognizing AI as a partner in the creative process, artists, innovators, and thinkers in all fields can reach a new level of expression and originality.

illution.biz

www.ingramcontent.com/pod-product-compliance
Lightning Source LLC
Chambersburg PA
CBHW071148240526
45465CB00024BA/2027